Self-Care for Hairdressers:

How to Prevent Stress and Burnout
and
Step Into the Professional You Were Meant To Be

Best Practices for Hairdressers, Vol. 1

Rebecca Beardsley

BizSmart Publishing
MARBLE FALLS, TEXAS, USA

Copyright © 2015 Rebecca Beardsley
Cover Design © 2015 Vanessa Mendozzi
http://www.behance.net/VANESSA31189
Book Layout © 2013 BookDesignTemplates.com

All rights reserved. No part of this publication may be reproduced, distributed or transmitted in any form or by any means, including photocopying, recording, or other electronic or mechanical methods, without the prior written permission of the publisher, except in the case of brief quotations embodied in critical reviews and certain other noncommercial uses permitted by copyright law.

BizSmart Publishing
701 US Highway 281, Suite E #1001
Marble Falls, TX 78654
support@bizsmartmedia.com

Self-Care for Hairdressers: How to Prevent Stress and Burnout and Step Into the Professional You Were Meant To Be/Rebecca Beardsley. -- 1st ed.
ISBN-13: 978-1519765642
ISBN-10: 1519765649

Disclaimer and Terms of Use: Effort has been made to ensure that the information in this book is accurate and complete; however, the author and the publisher do not warrant the accuracy of the information, text and graphics contained within the book due to the rapidly changing nature of science, research, known and unknown facts and internet. The Author and the publisher do not hold any responsibility for errors, omissions or contrary interpretation of the subject matter herein. This book is presented solely for motivational and informational purposes only. The Publisher has strived to be as accurate and complete as possible in the creation of this book.

While all attempts have been made to verify information provided in this publication, the Publisher assumes no responsibility for errors, omissions, or contrary interpretation of the subject matter herein. Any perceived slights of specific persons, peoples, or organizations are unintentional. For more information, please visit http://www.BizSmartPublishing.com

ENDORSEMENTS

"As I read this book, I found aspects of myself-my personal and professional behavior-on almost every page! Rebecca offers great insights and solutions in her book that are easy to understand. She makes us aware that in order to care for others we must take the time to care for ourselves! A must read."

~~Marlene Arce | Vice President, Education | L'Oréal Professionnel/Kerastase/Shu Uemura Art of Hair USA

"As hairdressers, I am always amazed by how much we give and share with others. We are the only professionals dedicated to improving the lives of others inside and out. We are all so passionate about our careers that few of us take the time to appreciate ourselves and check in with our own needs. Some may understand the importance to do this while others may not know what resources to turn to. Rebecca has now taken the mystery out of how we can care for ourselves so we can continue to thrive in our careers. Her years of experience, knowledge, and caring nature is a much needed dose of wisdom and medicine for all in the beauty industry."

~~Pepper Pastor, Director of Education ghd North America

"Now and again a book comes along to speak to the challenges that we in the beauty industry face and provide us with meaningful solutions. Rebecca's book falls into that category. Buy it, buy two and gift well-being to you and a friend."

~~James Morrison, Morrison Atilier

DEDICATION

This book is dedicated to the hairdressers all over the world who stand behind the chair, day in and day out, and who desire more meaning in their lives and want to elevate their job into a vocation.

ACKNOWLEDGEMENTS

Thank you to all my clients who have not only helped me be the hairdresser I am today, but continue to inspire me to be an even better artist and to own my expertise. It is a complete pleasure to serve you.

Thank you to the love and support of my friends, Elizabeth Nelson, Naomi Saks, and Mary Anne McKearnie. Thank you to Donna Gunter and BizSmart Publishing who have helped me birth the idea of this book and bring a dream into reality.

I'd also like to thank all the artists and leadership at L'Oreal Professionnel, who help me grow in such ways that I couldn't have imagined. I am forever grateful and honored to get to work alongside you, and for all the opportunities to grow as an industry artist and leader. Special thanks to Pepper Pastor, James Morrison, Marlene Acre for saying "yes." You are all artists I look up to and I deeply appreciate your support.

And last, but not at all least, to my loving husband Greg, and lovely daughter Pria, who never openly begrudge the suitcases when they appear in the living room, or the wefts of hair laid out over all the surfaces when it's time to do another shoot. You are truly my rock, and I can't imagine living my life without you. You help me be the person I want to be.

TABLE OF CONTENTS

Chapter 1: The Stress of Hairdressers 1
Chapter 2: Recognizing Burnout 9
Chapter 3: Impact of Hairdresser Stress on Clients 15
Chapter 4: Working Through Stress 19
Chapter 5: Practicing Self-Care 23

INTRODUCTION

Contrary to popular belief, hairdressing is a very stressful job. Hairdressers are trusted to help people with their image and help them feel better about themselves. I meet hairdressers all over the country who work really hard, yet they have lost their way creatively or are burned out and unhappy, wondering if they should do something else to make a living. They make very little money, and they move from salon to salon, hoping the next position will be better. Hairdressers do all sorts of things to control the anxiety, depression and anger in this very demanding career choice. This book focuses on what they don't teach in beauty school.

In these pages, you'll discover:

- Why many stylists leave the industry, burned out and underpaid, even though they may be booked in the salon.
- Why a lot of stylists are exhausted and losing sight of their hopes and dreams for their life.
- What they don't teach you in beauty school.
- Ways to manage stress, recognize the signs of burnout, start to dream again, and reconnect with your purpose, joyfully discover the professional that you were meant to be, and make the money you deserve.

Enjoy the journey!

Rebecca Beardsley

FREE GIFT FOR READERS

As a bonus for my readers, I'd like to offer you a free gift. My free report, 5 *Amazingly Simple & Effective Self-Care Strategies that Will Lead Hairdressers to a More Joyful Career*, is available for download at http://www.HairDresserSelfCare.com

Most Master Hairdressers know the importance of taking care of themselves as a hairdresser, and at one point or another realized how simple self-care strategies are crucial to their personal and professional growth.

Through my 30 years of experience in the fashion and beauty industries, I've personally seen the value of self-care. Download this free report to discover your chances of growing your career with joy, abundance, and deep meaning.

Get your copy today at http://www.HairDresserSelfCare.com.

ONE

THE STRESS OF HAIRDRESSERS

There's a big secret in the hairdressing industry that no one wants to discuss. That big secret is that being a hairdresser is stressful.

It's something we don't hear about and it's not something that hairdressers really talk about because we are in the profession of making people look good. Consequently, we're on the spot and need to look the part ourselves and act like we have it all together, even when it is a detriment to ourselves, and even if it is not true. We constantly give and keep little for ourselves on a spiritual, physical and emotional level, and sometimes even on a financial level.

Hairdressing is a very challenging profession because in school they simply teach us to pass a test. What isn't covered in school are the topics of psychological, physiological, and spiritual wear and tear on our bodies as well as in our hearts if we do not have a strong center. They don't teach us how to build a strong foundation of well-being to fortify ourselves in a number of ways so that we then can give all day long. They don't tell us we may run into psychologically unwell customers, or people who take and take, or work with people who are downers.

Years ago when I first started in the industry, I had lots of fear and trepidation about the career that I chose, or better yet, chose me. In short, it certainly wasn't love at first sight. In fact, my relationship with the industry was a very mixed bag at best. I worked hard, but couldn't make enough money to pay my bills, so I left the business and honestly didn't know if I'd ever return. I also didn't have the luxury of a family to depend on for financial support. I ran as far from hairdressing as I could. My story was certainly not the typical passionate, lifelong love story with my career.

Somehow, I always managed to have the confidence to find jobs, so I took a job to work at a fruit stand and became a manager very quickly. This job change satisfied my need for something different. I was still cutting hair but doing it out of my apartment, and the money I made from both allowed me to pay my bills. However, I didn't feel like this path was a long-term solution to having a career, but wasn't sure that salon life was my solution, either. A year later, a dear friend who managed me in my last salon job, walked into the fruit stand and said, "What are you doing? You're a hairdresser, for God's sake! Come with me and work at my salon."

That job lasted fourteen years, and Ron Shaffer, the owner, became one of my first mentors and dear friend. One of the things I noticed in the first seven years was just how much drugs and alcohol existed in the industry. It took some time for me to realize how those things became a way of life for me and many I knew and how much those issues negatively impacted our lives. We never thought to discuss the underlying issues of the demands our industry made on our lives, and we silently suffered together.

The issues range from the pressure of needing to look good to being empathic and having no boundaries, being trained to never say no, dealing with competition within salons, dealing with clients' vulnerability, creating on demand, keeping on schedule, making enough to live on, taking on client stuff, and playing psychologist, to name a few. Did you ever hear about these topics in beauty school? I sure didn't!

Self-Care for Hairdressers

What we take on as hairdressers while standing behind the chair can be very exhausting on all levels. In addition to dealing with things in our own lives, we also deal with what our clients are feeling and what they're going through in their lives. A hair salon is known to be a place where people talk, and I have a theory about that. When we touch their heads and the client is looking in the mirror, I feel like something happens in that moment. The client may do a mental or emotional dump of everything they are experiencing but be completely unaware this is what they are doing. Some of the information they share may be just a psychic drain and even depression can flow out of them without them saying a word. Most hairdressers I know are heart-centered folks, and we pick this stuff up without even realizing it, leaving us drained at the end of a day.

If you are new in the industry, it can be difficult to pick up on when this is happening and understand fully what is going on. That makes is very easy to unwittingly take on their stress, while the hairdresser is dealing with her own stressors of being on time, being a salesperson, being great at what we do, coming up with a plan to navigate a haircut, and then finally be creative on the spot, all the while your feet are killing you because you just had to have those cute shoes, but knew they were not right for the salon.

I think there's many aspects to why it is a stressful job and depending on where you work, it can be even more stressful. When my friend dragged me out of the fruit stand, I still held out for that something else that was my true calling. I bet if you talk to any hairdresser out there, they're always seeking something else. I would venture to say is it because they haven't found meaning in what they are doing.

Hairdressers are my heroes. There are many of them who are unsung heroes who don't work on celebrities, who may not have a mentor or someone to guide them, who stand behind the chair day after day, who don't get mentioned, who maybe get a thank you from their clients, but they're helping people look and feel beautiful. We need more beauty in the world and so I'd like to help hairdressers own what they do and become more of who they are behind the chair and find ways to manage the stressors in our industry. I want to help them unpack these issues and talk about the stuff we don't talk about and certainly they don't talk about in beauty school. That's where I'm coming from about this.

There are a couple of huge stressors for stylists.

Competition

Competition can exist between stylists in the salon, inside ourselves, with other salons, and even clients, if not checked. Healthy competition helps us be better at what we do and create a healthy culture for improving morale. However, too many times it's the survival of the fittest, and it can become a nasty nest of drama and set a tone of negativity, bringing down a salon.

I'd say a large percentage of hairdressers are perfectionists. We're harder on ourselves than most of our clients. The need to be on top of our game is real, because clients are very well-educated now, but this can also be driven by fear. Clients have begun to educate themselves about services and products, so stylists need to be very up-to-date on everything, from their look to what they're doing to technique to better products.

So, how can we balance being educated and professional without resorting to snarkiness with our co-stylists and salons? I believe there is enough business for everybody if we develop ourselves. Much of the training out there is technique-oriented, but

I want to talk about what's underneath the techniques because that is where the juice is, where true transformation lies, if we are willing to do the work.

Emotionally Available

Another stressor is the pressures of our lives outside the salon. Life can be intense as well as unrelenting sometimes. Our sister dies, our landlord gives us the boot, or our cat is sick. The stress can mount so high sometimes that you just don't know how you are going to manage going into the salon. Believe me, I've been there. I've experienced dark times where I don't even know how I showed up and cut hair.

Emotionally available?! Hah! That wasn't even a concept I could begin to grapple with until I had many years of therapy. Honestly speaking, I thought my clients were there to take care of me! I leaned on them, and so the boundaries were murky. The drama has to be put aside before we enter the door, as it competes for our attention at work, drains us, and oozes all over everybody, including our clients.

It's almost a "have to" to be available to our clients, be able to serve them in the way they deserve and respect them. I would even venture to say that until you are willing to grow, you will be stuck in a "job" versus beginning to change your job into a vocation. We need to put our own stuff aside so that we can be available to our clients, ourselves, and our team. Believe me, your "stuff" will be right there when you step out the door to go home.

Taking on Client Baggage

Taking on a client's baggage can be another stressor, and can certainly take the joy out of what we do. Being their therapist can be a very seductive and a slippery slope, especially in the beginning of our careers. Setting boundaries is a huge issue that we don't hear much about, yet is the brunt of many jokes in the industry. How can we preserve our boundaries while being fully present with the clients, but keep it professional? If we are going to raise the perception of our industry, it all begins with us as hairstylists.

Taking on the client baggage is one thing portrayed by hairdressers in the movies (think Steel Magnolias or Beauty Shop), and obviously that's based, in part, on real life. Beauty salons used to be places where community would come in, find out the latest news, and gossip. Many hairdressers know a wide range of things because of the people that come and sit in their chairs.

I'm the first to say my clients have educated me. They've taught me about the world. For a naive, young girl out of Redding, California, this was very eye-opening. It was a way of finding out about the world for me - it was my college education. Salons used to be places of gathering and knowing, and we don't have to lose this quality. How can we promote this feeling of community without us delving into the personal lives of our clients and becoming their therapist? Now, all I want to do is the job for which they are paying me - to cut, color, and style their hair and to be their beauty expert.

Some salons, on the other hand, can be almost be too beautiful or too sterile. They don't invite clients in to become a part of their culture. They lack the "soul" that welcomes the client into a safe haven to relax and to get comfortable being themselves when they walk through the door.

There are hairdressers who really delve in and try to find out everything about their clients, and I know a few who have lost their way by doing this. Most hairdressers are pretty empathic. Years ago, a very dear friend with whom I worked side-by-side for many years was the most empathic person I ever knew. He gave and gave and gave. He dug into the personal lives of his clients and shared very personal things with his clients and his clients returned the favor. In a short time, it became extremely draining and no fun at all. My dear friend absorbed a great deal of his client's baggage, saved nothing for himself, and twenty years later had a breakdown and had to leave the industry.

To be a master hairdresser, you don't have to go there. There's a way to take care of your clients without being their therapist. You want to be their cheerleader, and you tell them things like, "You look fabulous! That blouse looks beautiful on you!" It's not manipulation nor superficial. Mean it! Find something you appreciate and let them know. Sometimes this is the only positive feedback they receive all day. It truly is finding the gift that they bring in and highlighting it and make it the focus of your interaction.

Let clients find their own therapists, and start debunking the myth that that is your role. Be their cheerleader, without getting sucked into the drama. It took me a long time to realize that my clients don't want to hear about me. They want to talk about themselves, or not talk at all, and they want to be served.

TWO

RECOGNIZING BURNOUT

How do stylists recognize when they're experiencing burnout or stress? Sometimes it may just be feeling bad and feeling overwhelmed, but there are other signs that they should be mindful of.

Signs of Stress

Stress can be very subtle. Being stressed is not like you reach some road or holy ground, and then you're finished and you never work on these issues again. These issue will come up in your lives and throughout your career. It's not a one-stop-shop. It is something we continually need to work on, and I still do. There are ways we can recognize it. If you're feeling kind of sad or depressed when your client leaves, that's a concern. Start to notice how you feel when you're with the client. Are you giving so much that you have nothing left at the end of the day? At the end of the day we should feel as delighted as when we walked in the door, assuming we walk in the door delighted.

You also need to clear yourselves in the morning. I share that in my strategy tips on my website, http://www.HairdresserSelfCare.com, because it is something we continually need to work on, and there's ways we can deal with that. Another way of noticing it is if we feel defensive or if we feel anxious or apathetic. Perhaps we are feeling like we just don't care -- you are just doing your job. What I'm talking about is elevating ourselves so that we become masterful at what we do. It's about changing our job into a vocation. You really want to foster this career into something you really care about. If you do this, you'll be booked so much that the line goes out the door because your clients get when you care.

If you're feeling exhausted, lonely, isolated or just fed-up, you lose the ability to see and feel your vision for your life. You've lost your dream. Those are definitely signs of burnout and stress. I didn't really get that there was something greater for me in this industry until fifteen years in. They say it takes ten years to fifteen years to feel masterful at what you do, but that's about the time I went away to India. I was there six weeks when suddenly I started remembering a story about my sister putting makeup on me for the first time. At the end of the session, she put her hands on my shoulder and said, "Don't you look wonderful?" This experience sent a shock wave through me and made me ask, "Is that why I'm in this industry? Was that moment so powerful that I wanted to recreate that experience for clients?"

That's when I really understood there's something very profound here that I didn't need to run from anymore. I am proud to be a hairdresser and I truly want every hairdresser to feel that and own that. Recognizing those steps early on and dealing with them is going to just empower you to make changes in your life. You have a career that supports you and the way you need to do it.

Recognizing Stress

There are so many ways to recognize stress in ourselves and others. Sometimes it's just a matter of watching our co-workers and having our behaviors mirrored back to us. It's my belief that whatever is happening in our environment is a direct reflection of what may be going on for us. This industry is full of large egos which quickly grow out of control and get in the way of growth. Observing our behaviors can be insightful about what is going on in our internal world. Perhaps you are angry all the time or frequently lashing out at others. Perhaps you work with somebody who is just so defensive and she is hard to connect with. Maybe they blame others for their woes and for what's not going well. Maybe alcohol and drugs have affected you or those you love or your coworker or owner. Drugs and alcohol are a huge issue in our industry, as we love a big party! But this alcohol and drug habit, when left unchecked, can have a really negative impact on everybody.

We can be careless. It's very hard to stay centered and grounded in this profession that's so powerfully artistic and demands so much of us. We can be out of touch with how we feel, and short with both co-workers as well as clients. If you are not fully booked with clients, that is a sure sign of something happening and may be time for self-inventory. This situation may indicate that we are in a period of needing to grow rather than looking upon that situation as something we are doing wrong.

Perhaps you are over-eating, drinking coffee all day or consuming lots of sugar and wondering why you feel bad at the end of the day. I hate to break it to you, but these behaviors are leading to an unhealthy lifestyle, and I'm sure I'm not even capturing all of them. Sometimes I think hairdressers have this arms-folded attitude, which sends out a negative signal of, "What do you have to prove to me?" They're know-it-alls, so they can't let in a little bit of light and a little bit of breathing room for themselves. They are people who are usually giving way too much or not enough, and they don't typically have a very clear head.

How Stress Impacts a Stylist's Work

There are various ways stress can impact our work. Stylists can think that the salon is their own private stage so they get to just act out in different ways, and they do. Their clients are captive, and they can't move. The client has wet hair and can't just say, "You know, this is way too much. I'm going to walk out the door." Instead, the client just takes it, and then you don't see them again. I think that stylists can lose clients from not being on track with the fact that they work in a service industry. I think that stylists can become more talkers rather than listeners. A great quality to have as a hairdresser is the ability to listen and separate themselves enough to be a good listener. What is the client saying? And then remember these things about them when they walk in again.

Maybe the hairdresser starts acting snarky and is a little testy with their clients. I've been guilty of that. I have to catch myself and remind myself, "I'm here for them." It doesn't mean let them walk over you. It's having a healthy sense of boundaries and there's much to do there in terms of those boundaries. I think hairdressers can also be impacted by stress by becoming very defensive to feedback from their clients. Really, isn't that what this is about, is serving the clients?

The clients need the room to be able to say, "This really doesn't work for me," and the hairdresser not take it personally. It's just feedback on the haircut. It's not feedback on me, Rebecca the Stylist. Being defensive and not being able to hear our clients when they have criticism or feedback about their style or what you've done is a big sign. It's not personal.

I'm going to raise my hand and call myself out here. On the other side of that is a scenario where we give our power away all too often in the chair, relying on the client's sense of what looks good rather than owning our education and expertise. This was huge one for me and took me years to understand. It became extraordinarily stressful to continually fail to give myself credit and give voice to my knowledge. Eventually, this mindset became very detrimental to my well-being. My beliefs that I didn't know enough, along with my fear the client would see right through me, and my decision to just wing it through many a haircut just to try and give them what they wanted caused me untold stress. This denial of self and friction within can take an incredible toll on the body! And if you are in a high end salon, then the stakes are even greater, as it's your reputation as well as the salon's reputation on the line. It's enough to make the faintest of heart run full on in the other direction!

This opens a deep well of exploration for stylists. How we can raise our prices if we don't feel good about our work, or feel we are at a very base level and undeserving? Are we ever going to feel like enough? Then we start feeling resentful because we're not getting paid for what we do, and we can't pay our bills. We start taking our frustration out on the clients. It all begins with how we give our power away and by not being professional and not acknowledging our experience and education and directly telling the client, "This is what I think will look good on you."

When we feel we don't have power, we become very weak and we can feel caged in. It's a terrible conundrum, and we need to discover how to move out of that. We start feeling disconnected - from people, from reality, from our co-workers, from the salon. We become gossipers. Walk into some back rooms of salons, or even your own and you'll be amazed at what you hear! It is tough to remain positive in the thick of this and can be a losing battle. It's a bad reputation that salons and stylists have, but I think sometimes it's deserved. How do we move out of that? How do we raise the bar for ourselves and for those around us? It takes one person at a time. It takes one hairdresser changing her M.O. and it affects everybody out there in the industry. I feel like it has to begin with us. That's why I have started this book series on self-care. It all begins here.

When this sort of scenario is happening in our work, are we making money? Maybe some the stylists are bringing in a ton of money, but is that all there is? If we're having that experience in our daily lives, is that joyful? I can't imagine that it is. I think the price we pay is tremendous, and while we may not get it right away, at some point it catches up. This situation causes our spirit to become very small and defeated. I'm talking about breaking that up and bringing a much bigger game to your life and into the salon.

THREE

IMPACT OF HAIRDRESSER STRESS ON CLIENTS

A friend who lives in another part of the country recently related to me a story about her stylist who tells the same sad stories again and again about the stylist's derelict daughter and the daughter's derelict boyfriend every time my friend visits the salon. My friend said that she would become depressed after every visit, but still goes there, even though it's less frequently, because the stylist does a great job on her hair. But, my friend has to prepare herself for the onslaught of sad stories that she knows are going to be told. For real?!

It's like the client has to put on a shield to go in the salon. I have a client that cannot bear going into a big salon because number one, salons can be very intimidating. It's all about looking good. What if you don't look good when you go in? There is a tremendous amount of pressure to look great at all times. It becomes even more intimidating then when you've got all this drama going on in the salon between hairdressers. It can be pretty crazy. Loud music and all too hip people, tattoos everywhere and what if you're not that?

I think what happens is the client can start to feel very invisible, and there's nothing worse than people talking over each other and talking as if the clients aren't there. The clients are just sitting there in the chair like they're shrinking and you can see it. They sink down and feel very uncomfortable. Those clients, I can bet, you will not see again in the salon. If they're feeling talked over or feeling held captive, they feel unimportant, especially when every two minutes their stylist is getting a message that somebody at the desk needs them or the stylist is being interrupted for phone calls or delivery people. Salon owners can be quite guilty of this.

   Clients begin to feel like a number. The client begins to think that she is just a number in this cog of the wheel and has no interest in participating. They become unhappy and start to listen to friends who say, "You should come see my hairdresser! She is great." When the client leaves, the next time she'll visit her stylist's competition down the street, and the competition is great. There are many, many very skilled hairdressers who can deliver equal, if not better, work. Somebody will settle for mediocre work just to feel important. Stylists need to imagine themselves as the client. We have to check in with ourselves to see how our behavior is impacting our clients.

   It doesn't take much. We're great at perceiving what's going on with the client and what's going on with their hair. We're doing all of this in minutes, but are we really stopping long enough to see how our behavior is impacting them and their experience in the salon?

   I have almost thirty-five years of experience in this industry, and just yesterday I was thinking about one of my staunchest clients who has been with me twenty-five years. She's so beautiful with her sparse white hair and she still rocks a bob. She still comes to me and that means more to me than most things. It's that she has the sense of loyalty, and that's what we have the ability to engender. I'm not sure what impacted her twenty-five or thirty years ago when I was a kid in the industry, but that's what we can cultivate. It's that kind of long-lasting relationship that's very unique.

Today it's much more difficult to hold onto a client, especially for younger stylists that are used to moving around and changing salons on a whim. As I have learned, you take "you" wherever you go. What are we going to do differently to keep our clients in our chairs? It's not only feeling whole, complete and masterful at what we do. It's also by being masterful in the relationship and keeping our clients in the chair and by understanding it's all about service.

FOUR

WORKING THROUGH STRESS

Now let's talk about how a stylist can work through stress. Some of these strategies come from a personal place for me because I've had the great opportunity to have many teachers in my lifetime. I've always been, if you will, on a spiritual path. I've been very open to hearing how people get to the meaning of life, so these strategies are things I actually do every day.

Some of the things that help are setting up some time for ourselves to just sit with ourselves and see what the heck is going on inside. Instead of feeling those feelings, we want to push then away, drown them out with alcohol, or eat another cookie and forget about them. It's very easy to put our self-care on hold. When we are giving so much during the day, it's imperative that we have time for ourselves to reflect, whether it's sitting quietly, or it's sitting with a pen and paper and writing down our thoughts or writing down our intention for the day.

Some people call this ritual morning pages. I just call it simply tuning in with yourself and reflecting on what you're grateful for. Gratitude is a thing we hear about, but there's something very valid about counting those gratitudes for our day and in our life. We have so much to be grateful for. I think when we're muddled in our head and our experience of life can be challenging, taking that moment to find what we're grateful for is very powerful, because then we start feeling instantly better about ourselves and our life and what we're going to bring into the salon that day.

It's kind of like creating your rudder for the day. It steers where you need to be and the direction in which you need to flow. It's kind of like getting in motion with life. From all these practices I've done over my life, it's the most powerful and the simplest, so I find that that's really helpful, even if it's twice a day. At the end of the day, I'll sometimes take a different book that sits by my bed and I'll write about those who rubbed me the wrong way and release that energy - just somehow release it and let it go. Actually, the words I say are "release it to love." I recognize this is hard for me and I'm going to just let it go. It's very powerful, and I to go to sleep with that cleansed heart, if you will. It really helps in my intentions for the next day.

Then I'll think about what I liked about my day. What did I like? What went well? You can see there's more of this input of positivity that's very, very powerful, and it starts to erase the negativity. I'm telling you that negativity takes so much more energy than this more positive, good stuff. For years, resentment held my spirit captive, eventually, we need to forgive those who have harmed us, if we want to move in a much more effortless way, and truly be free. It's much easier to be joyful.

I then think about those areas where I feel stuck, where there's something I'm genuinely blocked about. I write it down, as well as start writing down some changes that I can make. Just calling attention to it and writing things down helps get it out of our heads and our hearts. I also think that sometimes just breathing into it helps. Simply taking a breath and walking out the door from the salon at lunch break will make all the difference in the world.

Self-Care for Hairdressers

We need to stop multitasking. We're texting while we're eating lunch or while we are going through mail. We're having a conversation while posting on Facebook. This scenario begs the question: Are we doing any of these things well? Hairdressers are notorious for being the quintessential multi-taskers. Get out of the salon for a moment, breathe the fresh air, take a walk, and put down the phone. Re-energize yourself for the day. Go sleep in your car for ten minutes. Different things for different folks, but finding those ways that can help us feel re-energized in our day can be so helpful, and crucial for longevity. There is so much more to say here, and I do offer some additional tips on http://www.Hairdresser-SelfCare.com. You will be able to find different strategies there.

FIVE

PRACTICING SELF-CARE

There are any number of ways for a stylist to take care of himself or herself. Let's talk about my top three favorites.

I think first asking the question, "Am I happy? Am I happy where I'm at? Am I happy not just only in my career choice, but am I happy in my career, in my life, in my environment?" I think that's a powerful place to start and from there we can say, "All right. There's a meltdown here. There's a breakdown, so what can I do about it?" Finding that, to me, is the most respectful thing we can do for ourselves, Just tune in and ask, "Am I truly happy?" From there it's like dreaming big. It's having a vision for life and having a vision for our career. Many of us have stopped dreaming and don't even have one. Why is that?

Ask yourself, "Where do I want to be in my career in five years, ten years?" This is a beautiful, useful exercise that I never stop doing, truthfully. It gives ourselves room to really create in our lives. Whatever that answer is for you, it can't help but bring a smile to our face and to your client's faces and help us feel more like, "Wow! I have a right to be here and I have a right to be happy and to have a life worth living." I think it's super powerful. Continuing to create is our lifeline as artists, as creators. Our creativity can be so shut down from the heaviness of life, so how do we reconnect with that creativity? I think the answer is just giving voice to that. Writing it down. Dreaming. Painting it. Color it. Activities like these can't help but start to foster some light and life in ourselves again. There again, we might find laughter, the most powerful medicine of all.

I think of Jason Backe within our L'Oreal Professionnel family whose laugh I recognize from far away, and it brings a smile to my face and it reminds me that laughter is the most contagious medicine. Laughter always makes us feel so good. Of course, there's lots of other things we can do, but I think those are some of the ways that we can get started.

How to Prevent Stress

Having a life outside the salon is so powerful. We forget this when we're on the track of being really great at what we do and being the best. I think master hairstylists have really figured out. They take a walk on the beach. They put the career aside and they foster these other areas of their lives, like their family or people they love. They spend time with them. Having hobbies outside of our career and having these healthy routines in our lives to support us help as well. Because we as hairdressers give so much, we've got to find a way to give to ourselves, and hopefully some of these will resonate with hairstylists.

I think hairstylists will be able to really connect with, "Oh, yeah. I need to get better at this. It's going to serve my career." Standing on the other side of thirty years in this career, I can say honestly that these strategies and these techniques help me bring my whole self to what I do, so I'm not just limping along. This is the perfect career for me, and I would choose no other. These are some of the ways that people can reduce the burnout and stress and stay thriving in the career for many years to come.

How Dealing with Stress Helps Hairdressers

As someone who coaches and mentors hairstylists, I help stylists deal with their stress. When stylists deal with their stress, they start to connect with their dreams again. When I'm out there speaking and working with hairdressers, I help them rediscover the light that had them start this career in the first place, and re-ignite the passion. The passion for what we do is not only about technique or a great haircut; and it's not only about a million bucks. It's about, "Do I feel whole in what I'm doing?" I help hairdressers find their dreams and cultivate respect for what they do. When one person changes, everything around them can change. We can affect our environment, with blame and say it's the salon that's bad. Rather than blaming it on an external force, stop for a minute. Let's really check within ourselves again.

I think dealing with issues like stress helps stylists be more responsible, and answer the question, "Why am I here? That's right. I got into this because I love styling and I love helping people!" They start connecting with a bigger dream. What's next? What do I get to create? It's like running up to the salon door and saying, "Oh, yeah! This is my life and I love it." If nothing else, it's helping stylists reconnect with their love for what they do and connecting to the creativity and finding their own voice in what they do. It helps them be a better designer or colorist.

Dealing with their stress helps them in finding their own taste of hair color, finding their own signature styles and having clients come back to them because they're uniquely themselves. It's finding their unique gifts in what they do, because we all bring something so different and so beautiful to our careers. Then they really begin to flourish.

I do have more strategies available for hairstylists at http://www.HairdresserSelfCare.com where you can instantly download different strategies. They're really fun and helpful for you, making it easy to keep at your desk, or at your salon.

When you visit RebeccaBeardsley.com, you can also view and subscribe to my blog which contains up-to-date tips and information on becoming a Master Hairdresser. I look forward to your visit. I look forward to serving more hairdressers, witnessing their growth and transforming our industry.

About Rebecca Beardsley

A native of San Francisco, Rebecca has styled hair for over 30 years in the Bay Area. She remembers loving fashion at the age of eight, influenced by her mother and five sisters, all of whom had great style and propensity for artistic expression. Rebecca's mother sewed matching dresses for the girls, painted her nails, and could be described as a fashionista in Hong Kong in the 40's, where she was raised. Her sisters wore the latest fashions, styled their hair, and applied makeup. Her father's travels all over the world by sea piqued her interest in travel, customs, dress and hairstyles of other cultures.

Rebecca integrates all the early experiences of shape, color, texture and mood with a great deal of passion while creating beauty and collaborating with other like-minded artists. She provides makeup, and hair services on location for print and film. She is owner of ShineForth Salon, is a member of the National Artistic

Team, as well as a member of the Styling Council for L'Oreal Professionnel, leading and building courses in Hairdressing in New York City. She is also a member of the Professional Beauty Association (PBA).

WEBSITE: http://www.RebeccaBeardsley.com
FACEBOOK:
https://www.facebook.com/RebeccaBeardsley
TWITTER: https://twitter.com/RBeardsleyHAIR
PINTEREST:
https://www.pinterest.com/rbeardsleyhair/
LINKEDIN:
https://www.linkedin.com/pub/rebecca-beardsley/16/36/ab9

Made in the USA
Middletown, DE
09 June 2018